MW01245650

POETIC VIEW

BY **ALOHA RICK**

WRITERS REPUBLIC L.L.C.
515 Summit Ave. Unit R1
Union City, NJ 07087, USA

Website:	*www.writersrepublic.com*
Hotline:	*1-877-656-6838*
Email:	*info@writersrepublic.com*

Ordering Information:
Quantity sales. Special discounts are available on quantity purchases by corporations, associations, and others. For details, contact the publisher at the address above.

Library of Congress Control Number: 2023951085
ISBN-13:   979-8-89100-459-7   [Paperback Edition]
            979-8-89100-460-3   [Hardback Edition]
            979-8-89100-461-0   [Digital Edition]

Rev. date: 11/17/2023

A letter from the Author:

    My writing desire started February 14, 1980
With the writing of a poem, I did the morning I heard my grandfather passed, four years had passed to my senior year in high school when I started to really write poetry, then it stopped for quite a few years, it wasn't until I lost love and found it again that I was able to pick up my pen.

    It wasn't until then that I saw things in such a way that allows me to appreciate life and what it has to offer that I can write a poem on just about any subject.

    I've spent years writing poetry with a poetic point of view, trying to bring a sense of understanding to just about every subject and narrative that I and my audience can think of, I try my best to tell both sides of most situations often giving each side its own Poem with a poetic view, I've been questioned by various members of poetry groups from around the world whom are very well educated in this field, two of them being professors in universities, questioning where I was educated in poetry, I am self-taught in this area and over the past few years feel like I've honed and sharpened my gift in the art of poetry writing, I've taken on writing challenges and written many upon request from many people even given myself quite a few writing challenges, I've been met with controversy on a couple poems and gained respect when I present them with the poem that has already been produced and shared telling the other side of the story.

Thank you all for the support of Poetic View by Aloha Rick, with a Poetic view maybe we will all see things are not always just black or white, if we view in a different light,
Sincerely Yours
Rick Beyer Aloha

☆ SPECIAL PRESENTATION! ☆

OUR UNIQUE AND EXCLUSIVE MUSE REVIEW IS IN!
WITH OUR PROFESSIONAL EXPERT POETIC REVIEWER
David Goliath Crow

My introduction and explanation behind my analysis:

As an observer, my analysis of a poem or writing is based on several factors. Firstly, I examine the literary devices used in the piece, such as metaphor, personification, or symbolism. Understanding and interpreting these devices help me uncover deeper meaning and the author's intentions.

I also consider the structure and form of the poem or writing. The arrangement of stanzas, lines, and rhyme schemes can provide insights into the author's style or thematic choices. For example, a sonnet's rigid structure might convey a sense of constraint or control.

Furthermore, I analyze the language and diction employed by the author. The choice of words, their connotations, and any linguistic patterns help me discern the tone, mood, or emotions being evoked. This analysis helps to understand the overall message or theme of the work.

Context is another vital component of my analysis. Knowing the historical, cultural, or biographical background of the author can shed light on their motivations, influences, or intended audience. Examining the poem within its broader context can provide a better understanding of its significance.

Lastly, I consider my analysis in the context of the reader's personal interpretations and experiences. While my analysis provides an objective perspective, everyone's response to a piece of literature is subjective. Therefore, my analysis aims to encourage critical thinking and open discussions about the multiple possible interpretations of a poem or writing.

🏆WINNER🏆

☆ ☆Congratulations! ☆ ☆

Rick Beyer !

"9/11"

"American Heroes"

I bet they didn't know the Heroes that would come along, on a day that terrorism didn't belong.

I bet they didn't know when they took those Towers from the sky, how much the American flag would start to fly.

It wasn't a question when it came the time, for that fireman to take to the stairs and start to climb.

To the top of the towers they fought their way, I bet they didn't know the Heroes they would become that day.

People helping people they have never met, these are the heroes we should never forget.

Firefighters, policemen and the common man, to become a hero this way is something you could never plan.

There are heroes that took over a plane, that saved so many others a grieving pain.

I bet they didn't know that on that day, the American people would have something to say.

When the dust started to settle and things became clear, I bet they didn't know American patriotism was something to fear.

It was a big price that some have paid, because there are easier ways for a hero to be made.

It didn't take long for it to show, when the American flag started to fly, it was time for terrorism to go.

Written by

RICK BEYER ALOHA

If you would like to follow me on Facebook: Poetic View by Aloha Rick

☆ SPECIAL PRESENTATION! ☆

OUR UNIQUE AND EXCLUSIVE MUSE REVIEW IS IN!
WITH OUR PROFESSIONAL EXPERT POETIC REVIEWER
David Goliath Crow

My free personal analysis as a prize for the winner of this activity:

This poem titled "9/11: American Heroes" by Rick Beyer is a tribute to the heroes who emerged on September 11, 2001, in response to the terrorist attacks on the World Trade Center in New York City. Let's examine what makes this poem praiseworthy.

1. Theme and Emotional Impact: The poem focuses on the heroism displayed by individuals amidst the tragedy. It captures the overwhelming emotions felt on that day and honors the brave actions of the firefighters, policemen, and the common people. The theme of courage, unity, and patriotism resonates strongly, evoking a sense of pride and remembrance.

2. Strong Imagery: The poem uses vivid and evocative imagery to convey its message. The description of the American flag flying amidst the chaos creates a powerful visual representation of resilience and national pride. The image of the firefighters climbing the stairs and the heroes on the hijacked plane highlights the bravery and selflessness exhibited by ordinary individuals in extraordinary circumstances.

3. Effective Use of Repetition: The repetition of the phrase "I bet they didn't know" creates a rhythmic structure and makes the reader reflect on the unexpected heroism that emerged from the tragic event. This repetition emphasizes the uncertainty of the heroes themselves, highlighting their selflessness and the unexpected turns of bravery.

4. Appreciation for Everyday Heroes: The poem recognizes not only the professional responders but also the "common man" who became heroes through their acts of kindness and support for strangers. This inclusive portrayal acknowledges the collective effort of individuals, emphasizing the power of unity and compassion.

5. Message of Resilience: The poem ultimately conveys a message of strength and resilience in the face of adversity. It acknowledges the heavy price paid and the lasting impact of the event but emphasizes the resolve of the American people to stand united against terrorism and to honor those who sacrificed their lives.

Overall, the poem is captivating and effectively captures the spirit of bravery, unity, and patriotism displayed by the heroes of 9/11. It pays tribute to their actions, ensuring that their selfless acts will not be forgotten.

🏆WINNER🏆

☆ ☆Congratulations! ☆ ☆
       Rick Beyer!

☆ SPECIAL PRESENTATION! ☆

OUR UNIQUE AND EXCLUSIVE MUSE REVIEW IS IN!
WITH OUR PROFESSIONAL EXPERT POETIC REVIEWER
David Goliath Crow

My introduction and explanation behind my analysis:

As an observer, my analysis of a poem or writing is based on several factors. Firstly, I examine the literary devices used in the piece, such as metaphor, personification, or symbolism. Understanding and interpreting these devices help me uncover deeper meaning and the author's intentions.

I also consider the structure and form of the poem or writing. The arrangement of stanzas, lines, and rhyme schemes can provide insights into the author's style or thematic choices. For example, a sonnet's rigid structure might convey a sense of constraint or control.

Furthermore, I analyze the language and diction employed by the author. The choice of words, their connotations, and any linguistic patterns help me discern the tone, mood, or emotions being evoked. This analysis helps to understand the overall message or theme of the work.

Context is another vital component of my analysis. Knowing the historical, cultural, or biographical background of the author can shed light on their motivations, influences, or intended audience. Examining the poem within its broader context can provide a better understanding of its significance.

Lastly, I consider my analysis in the context of the reader's personal interpretations and experiences. While my analysis provides an objective perspective, everyone's response to a piece of literature is subjective. Therefore, my analysis aims to encourage critical thinking and open discussions about the multiple possible interpretations of a poem or writing.

🏆WINNER🏆

☆ ☆ Congratulations! ☆ ☆

Rick Beyer !

Table of Contents

You're My Everything"

You are the rain that drowns my sorrow, the Sun that brightens my day, you're the force that keeps me going, along my lonesome way.

You are my coolness in the summer, my flowers in the spring, my peace my joy my happiness you're my everything

Written by

Rick Beyer Aloha

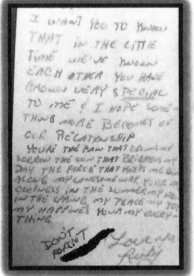

1984

1

"The Value of Time"

We should hope we never lose sight of its value or what it's worth, the value of time given to us from the time of birth.

It's value we must treasure because time never stops for use to measure.

The hands of time cannot by tide to slow it down, every second is accounted no extra can be found.

By the minute or by the hour it continues about its way, until we reach the end of each day.

Days become weeks that turn to months it now has been a year, where did time go? the answer is never clear.

Decades have passed as they start to mount, century after century we now can count.

In a box I don't think it will stay, on a chain and in our pocket still it gets away.

I've had it in my hand and still it I could not hold, that's when I knew time is worth more than gold.

Written by

Rick Beyer Aloha

"Rainbows Grow"

I always wondered I did not know, now I see, I see that rainbows grow.

They are rooted deep in the ground, a place that still has not been found.

It came to me in a dream, when from the ground I saw a beam.

Into this hole a took a view, I saw something I never knew.

It was beautiful and bright; I found the source of this beautiful light.

All the flowers that have ever grown, some look familiar, and a lot are unknown.

They come together in such a beautiful way; into rainbows they are put on display.

Brought to life by the rain and the sun, sharing its beauty when the storm is done.

At the end of a rainbow there is no pot gold, not like the story I've been told.

It was shared with me in a dream and now I know, there's a place in the ground where rainbows grow.

Written by

Rick Beyer Aloha

"Time Will Continue On"

I know, there will be a day the world will be letting go of what use to be, the world as we know it will no longer be.

When the time comes, I just want to say that I know.

The world is forever changing, trying to find its way, trying to make room for man getting in the way.

A fire burns and it clears the way, but man is here and, in the way, ahead of their time and in places they should not be, they saw it coming but they say it belongs to me.

We all are here on borrowed time living on lands that is constantly changing hands.

The history of mans troubled past is the sign that things will not last.

Man has traveled the distance beyond the horizon, now they have turned to the sky the stars are in

Here we are man and time have come face to face, time will win, and man erased.

Written by

Rick Beyer Aloha

"Until The Last Leaf Falls"

We sat here and I held your hand, this moment of beauty you just can't plan.

We shared the memories that we both could recall; of all the times we watched the leaves start to fall.

Each year was more beautiful than the last, when it starts to happen it happens way to fast.

You think these moments will last forever but they never do, the next time I do this it will be a memory for me, of you.

It's hard for me to imagine it feels really strange, that this will be the last time you will see the seasons change.

This moment was so beautiful one only you and I share, our last memory together while you were in my care

Let's sit here together so that one day I will recall, you and I sitting together and watching the last leaf fall.

Written by

Rick Beyer Aloha

"A Poetic Universe"

When I look at my surroundings it all looks so poetic to me, I start to write the words to describe what I see.

It could be a place of somewhere I've been, or a tattoo on someone's skin.

It could be the floating of a feather, or the changing of the weather.

It could be the moment when summer turns to fall or when winter turns to spring, you see for me it can be just about anything.

It could be the rising or setting of the sun, or it could be watching people have their fun.

It could be the waves that crash upon the beach, or it could be goals that people reach.

There is poetry in everything it's in the world in which we live, it's a gift I received from God and my words I intend to give.

Some see it as a gift others may see it as a curse, the way I see it we all live in a poetic universe.

Written by

Rick Beyer Aloha

"Crystal Ball"

As I look into my crystal ball, I could not believe what I saw.

I saw all the hopes and dreams that have ever entered my mind, I saw the sun rise and set and birds of all kind.

My ship set sail for a distant shore, taking me to places I've never been before.

Fulfilling the dreams, I forever had from my days that past, giving me hope for the future that will forever last.

Written by

Rick Beyer Aloha

"The Swan and The Princess"

Clad in the purest of white they bring beauty to our day, the swan and the princess finding their way.

Out of the darkness of the night, they found their way into the light

They walk among the waters as time begins to pass them by, beneath the stars in heaven beneath heavens sky.

So beautiful the swan and she in her dress, the beauty of them together the Swan and the Princess.

Written by

Rick Beyer Aloha

"It Leads to Nowhere"

The road I was on lead to the place of the hopes and dreams I once had, though my direction hasn't changed that road now leads to nowhere.

I will take to the ocean and set a course on the open sea and find my way by the stars I see.

The stars are no longer visible because of the condition the sky-is-in, I will keep moving forward in hopes that one day I reach the horizon.

The miles continued and the waters kept passing me day after day, the horizon never gets any closer nor does it ever get farther away.

It seems like I can't reach my destiny by land or sea maybe I need to take to the air, because it seems like my choice of travel leads me to nowhere.

Written by

Rick Beyer Aloha

"LOST AT SEA"

I WAS A LITTLE BOY, AND YOU, JUST A LITTLE GIRL WHEN WE PLAYED IN THE SAND, WAY TOO YOUNG TO SHARE A KISS BUT WE WOULD WALK HAND IN HAND.

YEAR AFTER YEAR OUR FAMILIES RETURNED TO THE SEA, I ALWAYS HOPED I'D FIND YOU LOOKING FOR ME.

TIME AFTER TIME TO MY SURPRISE, I'D FIND YOU STANDING IN THE MOST BEAUTIFUL SUNRISE.

WE SHARED A LOVE LIKE NO ONE HAS EVER KNOWN, AND INTO A BEAUTIFUL YOUNG LADY YOU HAVE GROWN.

NOTHING CAN REPLACE OUR MEMORIES FROM WAY BACK THEN, HOW SAD IT WAS WHEN OUR SUMMERS WOULD END.

I'LL NEVER FORGET THE YEAR WE NEVER CAME, THE SUNRISE TO ME WILL NEVER LOOK THE SAME.

WE FINALLY WENT OUR SEPARATE WAYS, HOLDING ON TO THE MEMORIES OF THOSE SUMMER DAYS.

ALL THESE YEARS LATER I NOW RETURN LIKE I DID SO MANY TIMES BEFORE, WITNESSING NEW LOVE FOUND ON THE DELMARVA SHORE.

I CAN'T HELP BUT WONDER WHAT COULD HAVE BEEN, IF OUR LAST SUMMER DID NOT END

I WILL ALWAYS FEEL OUR LOVE WAS MEANT TO BE I LIVE NOW FEELING LIKE OUR LOVE WAS LOST AT SEA.

WRITTEN BY

RICK BEYER ALOHA

10

"Fort Smallwood Rd"

Oh, how I love this old country road I traveled as a child, where time stood still and horses ran wild.

Thinking about our childhood the memories I see, the old gray house dad built high in top a tree.

Here we grew in so many ways, in a place where we shared our warm summer days.

As I walk toward the old dirt road memories I start to see, of a rope and tire hanging from the old oak tree.

If I could go back in time how wonderful that would be, to be that child again beneath that old oak tree.

We'd all be there brothers and sisters and our cousins to, never lacking anything to do.

Take me back to the place we traveled, to play on the road covered with gravel.

Written by

Rick Beyer Aloha

"Earth To Mankind"

I've been going in circles spinning around and around, if I should stop everything would fall to the ground.

You saw the warnings they were pretty clear, the climate has been changing year after year.

You have done more than scratch the surface you have broken through my crust, you give nothing in return, leaving behind, only your dust.

You have gone as far as the mantle trying to get at my core, I've been trying to tell you I'm growing tired, I'm getting sore.

You have trampled the forest and flattened the hills; my polar cap is melting now the river over spills.

You fight with each other in battles of war, I keep warming you I'm getting sore.

What does it take to get you to listen, and get you to see, the damage that you have done to me.

If you can't see the warning, you must be blind, please care for me, a message from Earth to Mankind.

Written by

Rick Beyer Aloha

"Armageddon"

The sun will rise, and the sun will set, and he will come again, a war between good and evil will bring this world to its end.

The day of judgement is upon us and is clearly coming into view, people are in turmoil not knowing what to do.

They gather the simplest of things then they start to hoard, people are secluding, and children are getting bored.

The enemy is here as it moves across the land, people want to stand and point instead of taking a stand,

Some will stand for nothing, and others will fall for anything at all.

Things are getting quiet as things begin to slow, I'm seeing a change in the people I thought I use to know.

It's been said the day will come when there will be fire in the skies, I didn't think I would see it coming from my neighbor's eye's.

The day of judgement is coming for those who wish to blame, you better choose your battle wisely and hope he calls your name.

Written by

Rick Beyer Aloha

"Between The Cold and The Rain"

I stood between the cold and the rain with no place to go, to add to my troubles the wind began to blow.

Trying my best to find my place, thoughts of my past in my mind begin to race.

I've been here and I've been there, it seems as though I've been most everywhere.

I've traveled far and beyond I've been as far as the horizon, I now have set my sights on the sky the stars are in.

It gives me hope to ease the pain, of all the times I stood between the cold and the rain.

Written by

Rick Beyer Aloha

"A Place to Call Home"

If it wasn't for this big, beautiful world I'd have no place to call home, grassy carpet I have for my floors, a big blue sky with puffy white clouds for my roof.

No door to place my number, and no place to hang my hat for proof.

Forest all around me I'll use for my walls, and for my shower I think I'll use the waterfalls.

The winter snow is my air condition, the sun I'll use for my heat.

If it wasn't for this big, beautiful world I'd have no place to rest my tired feet.

Written by

Rick Beyer   Aloha

"The Missing Piece"

It lies upon the floor near my feet, the missing piece that would make me complete.

With my hands upon my head my thoughts are my own, I sit upon a stool sitting all alone.

I'm starting to fall apart one piece at a time, as the clock upon the wall starts to chime.

As I begin to fall apart, I hope to rebuild with the love in my heart.

My falling apart will then begin to cease, for I have found the missing piece.

Written by

Rick Beyer Aloha

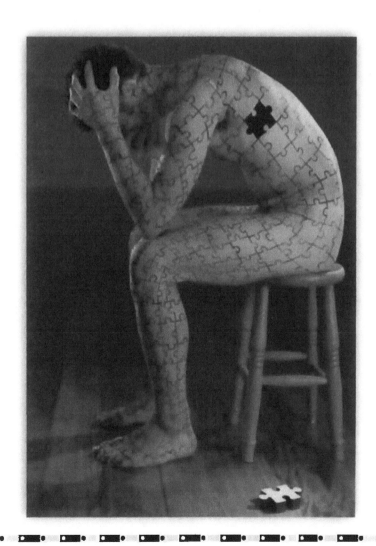

"And Then It Was Fall"

I stood atop the mountain early in the spring, I took it all in view and see the beauty in everything.

I stood there for just a moment and to God I pray, I thanked Him for such a beautiful day,

Off in the distance the sun begins to rise, God must be an artist because He paints such beautiful skies.

He does it with such grace with the just wave of His hand, in front of me I see life as though He had this planned.

The animals in the forest and the birds in the skies, all season long He has brought beauty to these eyes.

From the mountains I have traveled now I made it to the shores, I will now enjoy my summer with sand covered floors.

I watched it rise above the mountains now I'll watch it rise from the sea, I close my eyes and listen and pretend he shares this only with me.

It took me a lifetime to finally hear the eagles call, just like that spring became summer "And Then It Was Fall"

Written by.

Rick Beyer Aloha

Photo by   Lisa Johnson

"Where Did the Time Go"

I laid down to take a rest one day, and time just got away,

We start looking back and we always seem to wonder where did time go, we try to remember how did it get away sometimes we'll never know.

I start the think and then I start to see, time got away from me.

As I lay here, I begin to dream of all that is yet to be, I can only hope they become reality.

I dreamt of the future looking for time, for there are still some mountains left for me to climb.

At the top it may be lonely, and it may be cold, if we could only share our time for your hand I wish to hold.

Let's do this right because time is running out and things are growing old, please take my hand there's some things to you I'd like to show before we ask where did the time go.

Written by

Rick Beyer Aloha

"Urban Warfare"

No longer do I stand in the shoes I use to wear; no longer will I stand beneath the hat that covered my hair.

I will no longer hear the children that play in the street, no longer will I shake the hands of my friends when we meet.

I will not be able to comfort those that feel the pain, that caused their tears to fall like rain.

No longer do we need to be aware what we need now is for people to care, so we don't lose another to this urban warfare.

Written by

Rick Beyer Aloha

"Burning Bridges"

I have been the bridge for which others have crossed, and once they made their way aside, I was tossed.

I have given all of me only to learn, people think nothing of the bridges they burn.

I'm often left wondering how can one walk upon your back, and walk away like it was some sort of circus act.

I have also helped others reach to a greater height, while I'm left in the dark and they stand in the light.

The whole time knowing to make it alone they can't, and it isn't until then that we learn, that some people don't care about the bridges they burn

Written by

Rick Beyer Aloha

"A Snake in The Grass"

I was taught to fear what I could not see, the lion in the bush isn't what will devour me.

Be careful of those that slither in the grass, they crawl on their belly, so no shadows cast.

You will not see it coming they will catch you by surprise, you will feel their fangs then you paralyze.

Motionless you lay, swallowed like prey.

A snake in the grass will swallow you whole, leaving behind nothing not even your soul.

I kept my eye on the most feared of all beasts, not knowing that it, I should fear the least.

Hidden in seclusion just out of view, waiting for the right moment to strike upon you.

You won't see it coming it will happen real fast, attacked by a snake that lies in the grass.

Written by

Rick Beyer Aloha

"Who Shall Die First"

When the time comes who will it be, I hope that it is you and not me.

Let it be me to be the one to live with the pain, let it be me who cries the tears that fall like rain.

Let it not be you to find me or lay me in wake, let it not be you for there are final decisions to make.

Let it be me whom goes through your things, let it be me to deal with the pain it brings.

We have shared a life of love and happiness like no other, to live without that is a pain I wish for you not to discover.

Let it be me to visit the place for where you lay, let it be me to be carried to you on my final day.

I stayed behind and handled our final affairs, now I shall join you and climb the heavenly stairs.

Let it be me you greet at the pearly gate, a moment in time a moment of fate.

Written by

Rick Beyer Aloha

"The Toss of The Dice"

Used in many ways for centuries they've been tossed, games have been won and lives have been lost.

It's happened to many, more than once or twice, people willing to risk it all to the toss of the dice.

Let it ride you hear them shout, until it happens then their luck runs out.

Decisions are made often by the flip of a coin by calling heads or tails, more often than not winning always fails.

The gambler will chance it all, leaving the chips where they fall.

He is never willing to take any advice, thinking one day he will win and live in paradise.

The day will come he will become cold as ice, all because he lost it all to the toss of the dice.

Written by

Rick Beyer Aloha

23

"Inner Beauty"

Beauty was never bestowed upon me; some look the other way when they see what they see.

I wasn't much to look at my friends were very few, so I often tried to stay just out of view.

There is a beauty we all possess that we often hide, some don't see it until you look deep inside.

Into the heart is where we should look and then you will see, you will see the beauty the beauty of me.

It is often overlooked many a times I cried, why can't we see the beauty the beauty that hides inside.

Written by

Rick Beyer Aloha

"Fire In the Sky"

Something is different it isn't quite the same, it looks as though the sky has been set a flame.

As we witness a fire, we all can see, I can't help but wonder how this can be.

Clouds of fire cry like rain, I hope the ocean can douse earths pain.

The world is in trouble I can hear her cry, nothing left to burn there's now fire in the sky.

Written by

Rick Beyer Aloha.

"Holding Onto Summer"

The last day of summer I have tied to this rope, I don't want this to end is what I hope.

I've played all summer and had my fun, trips to the beach to play in the sun.

Holding onto this moment that I love best, soon will be replaced by a long winters rest.

Soon the leaves will change their colors and fall to the ground, winter will settle in oh what a peaceful sound.

Another year will pass that will allow me to grow, but for now I'll be holding onto summer trying my best not to let it go.

Written by

Rick Beyer Aloha

26

"American Heroes"

9-11 Tribute

I bet they didn't know the Heroes that would come along on a day that terrorism didn't belong.

I bet they didn't know when they took those Towers from the sky, how much the American flag would start to fly.

It wasn't a question when it came the time, for that fireman to take to the stairs and start to climb.

To the top of the towers they fought their way, I bet they didn't know the Heroes they would become that day.

People helping people they have never met, these are the heroes we should never forget.

Firefighters, policemen and the common man, to become a hero this way is something you could never plan.

There are heroes that took over a plane, that saved so many others a grieving pain.

I bet they didn't know that on that day, the American people would have something to say.

When the dust started to settle and things became clear, I bet they didn't know American patriotism was something to fear.

It was a big price that some have paid, because there are easier ways for a hero to be made.

It didn't take long for it to show, when the American flag started to fly, it was time for terrorism to go.

Written by

RICK BEYER ALOHA

"Freedom Tower"

Like a phoenix this tower has risen from the ashes and will stand forever tall, like an eagle may it stand strong and show the world never again will it fall.

Here we stand in the shadow of a time that has come to pass, in the shadow of a memory that will forever last.

Some may never have lost a loved one on the day the towers fell, but we have all shared in the loss just as well.

Let this tower of freedom be a memorial for the price that was paid, on a day that so many heroes should never have been made.

As we watch the freedom tower reach for the sky, let it be known that American patriotism will never die.

When patriotism and terrorism clash, like a phoenix we will rise from the ash.

Written by

Rick Beyer Aloha

"The Sky Is Falling"

I traveled to the ocean to watch the sunrise, but something was different that caught me by surprise.

The sun hasn't yet risen, something else came into my vision.

The sun was still laying below the horizon, when I noticed the condition the sky-was-in.

Things were really quiet the waves were the only sound, it started to appear as though the by surprise.

Wave after wave they rolled ashore, I can't help but wonder has this happened before.

I would not have believed it had I not seen with my eyes; I was here when the clouds fell from the skies.

They laid on top of the ocean then they gathered on the sand, I dropped to my knees and held them in my hand.

As I looked it appeared to me, it looked like the sky was touching the sea.

The sun started to rise the way God had always planned, but it makes me start to wonder why are the clouds laying on the sand.

Written by

Rick Beyer Aloha

"The Carousel"

I heard the last of the laughter as they scream and yell, the last of the joy that came from the carousel.

Slowly it would go around and around, the music stopped and then there was no sound.

No more children no more fun, the sound from the carousel is finally done.

One by one quickly they ran astray, trying their best to get away.

No longer could they stay on course, off and running ran the old wooden horse.

No one left, no one to tell, what has happened, to the old carousel.

Written by

Rick Beyer Aloha

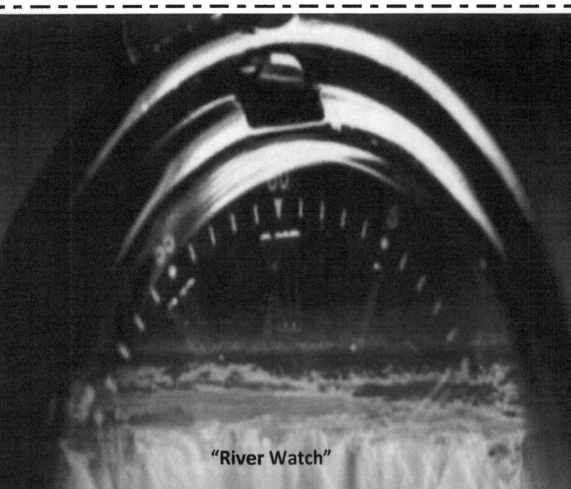

"River Watch"

Have you ever sat and watched the river flow, have you ever
 wondered where does it go.
I sat at the source, and watched it set its course.
It carves its way through my dreams, of me sitting on the edge
 of these mountain streams.
The river is so peaceful and serene, as if it's a part of its
 daily routine.
Carving its way making its notch, as I sit here, the river I watch.

Written by
Rick Beyer Aloha

"Sweeping It Under the Rug"

If you are going to take the time to do a job at all, do it well and stand proud and stand tall.

Don't waist the time of cutting corners to save some time, don't skip steps on the stairs you climb.

You may start to stumble you may even fall, and that is how you are remembered as people begin to recall.

A job worth doing is a job well done, if you not going to do it right it is better left undone

You may not care your shoulders you may even shrug, but don't be caught sweeping the dirt under the rug.

Written by

Rick Beyer Aloha

"Glowing"

It wasn't until I was broken that I started to glow, there was so much about me that even I didn't know.

Like a glow stick in the night, it has to be broken before you see it's light.

By the hands of God, I have been bent and broken, by his actions to me He had spoken.

Like a stick tied to a string, I didn't glow until I lost everything,

I had to be broken I had to suffer loss to fulfill my purpose in life to know the reason for my being, it wasn't until then that I was able to start seeing.

There are those that choose to just exist and there are few that are chosen to be bent and broken so they can see reality.

We suffer sickness but we survive, for there is a reason we are kept alive.

We lose jobs, we go through divorce but somehow we stay the course.

We have to bury our family and bury our friends, never knowing when it all ends.

In those final moments of desperation Is when we start knowing, why I was broken and started glowing.

Written by

Rick Beyer Aloha

"The Family Chain"

A bouquet of memories watered by a million tears, wishing God could have spare you a few more years.

We cannot bring back the days of old, all we can do is sit and listen when the memories are told.

Our memories of happier days gather in our mind, there they will stay like a world left behind.

As I think about all of the yesterday's, the ones I remember best a smile comes to my face, there is a silence in my heart that no human eye can trace.

Your last words to us all have been spoken, as we all try to keep it together the family chain is broken.

Written by

Rick Beyer Aloha

"I'll Never Let Go"

Holding onto to the love we'll share forever, a love in which I shall never surrender.

I will hold on tight and never let go, of a love that will forever grow.

If either I or you shall depart, our love will continue to live within our heart.

Shower me with roses cover me with the scent, embrace me with the love that was meant.

I will hold on to you forever I hope you know; our love is forever I'll never let go.

Written by

Rick Beyer Aloha

"Something I Can't Unsee"

You let me find you, I wonder why, I screamed real loud as I let out a cry.

Our love was brand new, now I have to go on without you.

You made a decision all on your own, did you give any thought to how I would be left all alone.

There are others more than just me, I wish you would have thought how lonely they will be.

Soon there will be many that will hear the news, but for some, it won't take long for someone else to fill your shoes.

But there are others that will be left with an empty space inside, you filled a place in their hearts that no other can fill, no matter how hard they tried.

I wish you could have seen what you were leaving behind, before you made a decision that was so unkind.

Did you not think of who it might be, I was the one who found you something I'll never unsee.

I can't help but wonder what was going through your mind, it now makes me wish, I wish I were blind.

Suicide awareness

Written by

Rick Beyer

"Forgotten Memories"

Dementia awareness

Sometimes when I look in the mirror I do not recognize the person looking back at me, but I see a resemblance of the person I used to be.

I may not remember your name, but my feelings for you are still the same.

It's scary sometimes because I don't remember where I am, but I will find Comfort if you would just hold my hand.

Memories of yesterday fade in and out, some days I remember and some days I have doubt

I treasure the good days when I can remember your face, and I remember our times in a happier place.

I know the good days will soon come to an end, the next time I see you I may not remember you as my friend.

Please remember me as I once was and please know that I have no regrets, my mind may not know you but my heart will never forget

Written by and in collaboration

Rick Beyer Aloha

Sandy Wilson

"A Letter from God"

I've been watching you for quite some time and your loneliness has caught my eye, I've been listening to you, and I have also heard your cry.

I've read the questions you haven't yet written in the sand; I will give you the answers if in mine you will place your hand.

Walk with me along life's way, I will give you the hope and faith that will brighten your day.

I will chase away all of your sorrows, so that you can have better tomorrows.

Walk with me and I will show you new horizons as we watch the sun rise from the sea; you can live a new life if you put your faith in me.

Keep your hope and faith and have no fear, as you watch this ink slowly disappear

P.S. Listen for the angels to sing your tune; keep the faith I'll see you soon.

Written by God

Through my hand

Rick Beyer Aloha

"When The Whistle Blows"

When we board the train for eternity, we shall pray we are on the right track, when the train gets going there is no turning back.

The train gets going along life's way, it will travel past the meadows that bring beauty to our day.

This train will travel through the hills near mountain streams, like the ones I see in my nightly dreams.

It will pass among the forest that grows trees real tall, as I ride this train my life I begin to recall.

I start to reminisce of the years that past, oh boy did they go so fast.

All the things I've ever done play slowly in my mind, as some of my memories become hard to find.

Eternity is forever how long that is nobody knows; we can only hope we are on the right train when that final whistle blows.

Written by

Rick Beyer Aloha

I Heard the Train Whistle Blow

"How Long Is Forever"

How long ago did it start it must have been forever ago, how long does forever last does anyone know.

We know that all things one day must come to an end, all except for time it will last forever and ever and forever and again.

We hold on to memories, but they too will not last, a lifetime to make them seems like forever but it to is gone real fast.

Life as we know it one day will not be, this we must except as apart of reality.

It does not matter how big it is, it too will one day crumble to the ground, it will happen to all things we see today then it won't be found.

Nothing last forever except time and space, a fact of life that we all must face.

Written by

Rick Beyer Aloha

"A MESSAGE IN A BOTTLE"

I was sitting on the beach when it became low tide, in the sand was a bottle with a note inside.

It brought back memories from a long time ago, when I wrote a letter, tide it to balloon and let it go.

I hoped someone would find it who needs someone like me, I hoped it would make it across the ocean and it not get stuck in top a tree.

Maybe this bottle came from across the sea, where some unfound love is waiting to be.

Maybe it came from a sinking boat, so I pulled the cork and read the note, and this is what I read.

I'VE BEEN WATCHING YOU FOR QUITE SOME TIME AND YOUR LONELINESS HAS CAUGHT MY EYE, I'VE BEEN LISTENING TO YOU AND I ALSO HEARD YOUR CRY.

I HAVE READ THE QUESTIONS YOU HAVEN'T YET WRITTEN IN THE SAND, I WILL GIVE YOU THE ANSWERS, IF IN MINE YOU WILL PLACE YOUR HAND.

NOW WALK WITH ME ALONG THE WAY, I WILL GIVE BACK YOUR FAITH IN ME, AND THE HOPE THAT BRIGHTENS YOUR DAY.

NOW TURN AND LOOK TOWARD A NEW HORIZON AND WATCH THE SUN RISE FROM THE SEA, YOU ALSO CAN LIVE A NEW LIFE IF YOU KEEP YOUR FAITH IN ME.

When I looked to see who signed the note.

"SINCERELY YOURS LOVE GOD," was whispered in my ear, as I watched the ink slowly disappear.

P.S. I GOT YOUR NOTE TIDE TO A BALLOON, I HOPE YOU KEEP YOUR FAITH SEE YOU SOON

Written by

Rick Beyer Aloha

41

"Like Dust in The Wind"

I blew them from the pages like dust, the words I was reading I could not trust,

They gathered in a cloud like rain, all the words that have been written inflicting it's pain.

Let the words upon my pages cause no harm to those who read, take from these pages the words so that you succeed.

Words of encouragement laughter and love, they do not gather in that cloud above,

Those you will find written on the pages in between, as if they were the lines of some romantic scene.

I blew from these pages all the words of sin, blew them like dust, dust in the wind

Written by

Rick Beyer Aloha

"The Phonebook"

I was sitting all alone, wanting to just talk on the phone.

I thought real hard and it came to mind I had no one to call, time stood still as it began to stall.

In that moment out of the corner of my eye it caught me by surprise, I then started to realize.

I have this book of numbers there surely must be, someone out there willing to talk with me.

The numbers seemed endless there was one after another, there were hundreds among thousands from cover to cover,

I opened the pages and started to look; I ran my finger along the numbers then closed the book.

Written by

Rick Beyer Aloha

"Hearing is Believing"

After today my life will no longer be the same if I don't respond to what you say my hearing will not be the blame.

I hope when you say something it's worth hearing, how I respond you may want to start fearing.

I spent my life living in a world that the things I heard were not always clear, it wasn't that I wasn't listening or that I didn't care, I just couldn't hear.

There were many, that never knew, please understand I was not ignoring you.

Please know how good a listener I was, I did not ask you to repeat yourself just because.

I had to listen real hard, so I could hear every word, way too often there were things I never heard.

It took me a lifetime but it I finally found; how beautiful the world is when it has sound.

The sounds of the wind blowing in the top of tree will now sound a little different for me.

The sounds of the birds I can now hear, their singing and chirping to me is real clear.

The rivers running toward the sea, now has a whole new sound to me.

I can now hear the animals in the wild, I can now hear the cry of some young child.

After all this time I finally found, the world looks different when it has sound.

So, after today, watch what you say.

If you think I didn't hear your voice, that may have been by my choice.

Written by

Rick Beyer Aloha

"A Different Time A Different Place"

If I could go back in time and all my mistakes could be erased, all my steps would be carefully traced.

They will lead to a place in time much like today, when our love was trying to find its way.

Time and distance separated then and now, here we are still trying to love each other if only time will allow.

We were high school seniors way back then, here we are seniors in time trying to love again.

You're still just as beautiful as the day we met, a moment in time I'll never forget.

Time for me has had its way, as I am now broken and gray.

All these years later we never knew that you loved me, and I still loved you.

Now here we are nearing our final day, once again our love is trying to find its way.

I can still remember the first time you placed your hand upon my face, it was a different time and a different place.

Written by.

Two less lonely people

Rick Beyer Aloha

"Hunger - It's Not Artificial"

If everything around us is no longer real, how come hunger some can still feel.

There are things we taste and if it you wish to savor, soon it will become an artificial flavor.

Even our fish, hamburgers, and steak, have now become fake.

They will look you in the face and tell you it's ok its plant base.

Soon we won't know how to act, even your feelings will be an extract.

You have brought to us artificial intelligence so now we no longer need to think, our world is out of order our timing is out of sync.

You brought to us artificial reality with goggles we now can wear, so we can see things that are not really there.

You brought to us artificial flavor to satisfying our taste, soon everything will be gone lost without trace.

But still, we are here let's make this official, the feeling you get from hunger is not artificial.

If you need something to look at this is what it should be, there is no artificial hunger it is reality.

Written by

Rick Beyer
Aloha

"In Search Of"

I looked around the corner and I looked over the hills and I looked far away, I turned over every rock I saw and I dug deep into the earth, I could not find it anywhere until I started to pray.

I thought I had found it a couple of times but that was not true, I could not find love anywhere until the day I met you.

It's funny where you find it when it was there all the time, I searched for it everywhere, there were even mountains that I climbed.

I was looking for a diamond I thought I would look high up in the mist, I could not find it anywhere, so I crossed it off my list.

A diamond in the rough I thought I was in search of, I finally found my precious gem when I found your love.

Written by

Rick Beyer Aloha

"Trains/Trains"

They crisscross going here and there every day, their whistle blows as they make their way.

Pulling their loads across tracks of steal, this old iron horse replaced the wagon and wheel.

Mighty and powerful they struggle with ease, pulling the freight to settle our needs.

Across the land they travel to deliver their goods, crossing rivers and mountains through tunnels and woods.

Some are loaded with freight of all kinds, food and beverage tractors and coal, powered by diesels until they reach their goal.

Fruits and vegetables flour and grain, brought to us all by the power of the train.

Written by

Rick Beyer Aloha

"Sunflower Fields Forever"

As I stand here and dwell amongst the ruin, I see fields that sunflowers once grew in.

Blue skies above of a calmer day, fields of yellow, in the breeze they sway.

Sunflowers grow in a place of joy, a place I use to play as a little boy.

Above me now the skies are gray, as I fold my hands to God I pray.

Bring back the peace we once knew, bring back the Sunflowers that once grew.

Bring back the yellow, bring back the skies of blue, bring back the peace and joy we once knew.

Memories I have they will leave me never, let us stand in sunflower fields forever.

Written by

Rick Beyer Aloha

"Save Time for Me"

Don't close your eyes before you tell me good night, I'll sit here and wait before I turn out the light.

There's something that I know it's so easy to see, before this life ends will you save time for me.

We've had time together, but we never woke to the rising sun, a dream I hope to share before this life is done.

Before you close your eyes and turn out the light, do you think of days of me holding you all night.

If ever I hold you in my arms there's something, I wish for you to know, I'll hold you forever and never let you go.

I keep holding on the same way that you do, in hopes of one day I'll wake up next to you.

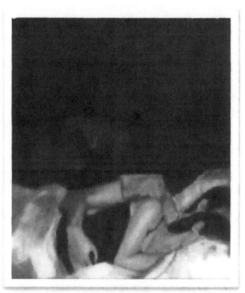

I know we share the same dream in hopes that day can be, before this life is over will you save time for me.

If someone is going to hold you let it be me tonight, let it be me that leans over and turns out the light.

Let me hold you darling let me be the one to listen to your cries, put your head my shoulder and just close your eyes.

I'll take away the sorrow of what makes you cry, let's wake up together and watch the sun rise into the sky.

When we are together think how this love has grown, with me you'll find more love than you've ever known.

I hope that one day this you will see, before this life is over will you please save time for me.

Written by

Rick Beyer Aloha

50

"The Hourglass"

Some measure in minutes some measure in days, our time together we measure in many ways,

My love for you is measured by each grain of sand, from the very first moment that I held your hand.

As we look into the hourglass there is a couple that I see, I can see you growing, growing old with me.

Let the sand begin to fall and gather in the glass below, let it measure the years we shared and hope they fall real slow.

Let's walk through life together hand in hand, and in this glass of time together we will stand.

In this glass of time the sand will start sieve, and each grain of sand will measure all the love I have to give.

If love is our time of measure forever, we will live.

Written by

Rick Beyer Aloha

"Through The Lens"

I view this world through the eye of my camera as the day transforms, I've captured beautiful Rainbows after I capture the eye of the storms.

I've taken pictures near and far, I have taken them of the sun and the moon and of the most distant star.

I have captured moments by the fire and moments of the chill when it gets cold, I have captured the memories, so they never grow old.

I've captured the calmness of the waters that slowly passes by, I have captured eaglets in the nest and Eagles in the sky.

I've captured the most beautiful moments that don't seem real, moments of nature moments you can feel.

As I sit here and think of everything I saw, I start to realize my tripod is a fiberglass hull.

Written by

Rick Beyer Aloha

Photo by

David Sites

"Where Did All the Rabbits Go"

As I look out the window at the world outside, I can't help but wonder where did all the rabbits go to hide.

On my walk I occasionally see a rabbit or two, but then I started to notice there are none in view.

The forest is leveled now the grass won't grow, where for then will all the rabbits go.

The world is in trouble destroyed by mankind, the rabbits I used to see are now hard to find.

Can we not save this planet, for way too long we have taken things for granite.

The world is drowning by the tears I shed, I no longer see the rabbits I once fed.

Neighborhoods rise where the deer once grazed, as the rest of the world is set ablaze.

Man will run seeking higher ground, until one day we will listen and hear no sound.

We will then wonder but we will never know, where did all the rabbits go.

Written by

Rick Beyer Aloha

"Land and Sea"

I sat here staring through the window at the world outside, watching water and earth as they both collide.

One without the other we already know, Earth without water nothing would grow.

Water without land, we would have no place to stand.

They came together land and sea, that's how things came to be.

It does not take long for things to emerge, soon right after a tidal surge.

They embrace each other the way lovers do, and things start to be, nothing would exist no birds or trees no you or me, if it were not for the land and the sea.

Written by

Rick Beyer Aloha

"A Special Place in My Heart"

There is a special place in my heart where no one has ever been, and you take me their time and time again.

When I go there, I see all the things that I ever wanted, and if just one of them came true, I would choose the one that my life only involves you.

When I lay down at night all the dreams, I've ever had enter my head, I look over at you because of what you just said.

When I heard you say I love you it made me start to cry, I can't believe we are both laying here, baby you and I.

I will love you through the darkest of times, and protect you through the darkest of night, I'll love you forever and hold you close until we see the morning light.

I feel like when I'm with you, that at least one dream came true.

I want to share with you, the dreams That have not yet come true.

I have dreams of walking on the beach together you and I, we turn to each other and start to kiss as the sun falls from the sky.

Into the sunset we walked hand-in-hand, and somewhere along the way we stopped and wrote our names in the sand.

The biggest dream I ever had in my life, is the one where I have you as my wife.

I wish to share all the dreams I have and the final one too, before our lives are over, I want you to know that I love you through and through.

I want to let you know that when I'm with you, that my favorite dreams do come true, and one of my favorite ones, is when you are loving me, and I am loving you.

Written by

Rick Beyer Aloha

"The Blood of a Poet"

As I sit and write about the state of mind, I'm in, my words drip like blood of things I've seen and places I've been.

My words fall upon the paper and start to gather, they drip like blood as they start to splatter.

My flesh has become thin, my words are blood, and my paper is skin.

My heart is the ink well from where words flow, my flesh is my paper as they start to show.

As we start to write, shall we succeed, from these veins our words do bleed.

How we feel some may never know it, words are "The Blood of a Poet"

Written by

Rick Beyer Aloha

"A Poet Without Words"

What would a poet be without words, it would be like the sky without birds?

What would the forest be without trees, there would be no place for squirrels or honeybees?

What if the desert had no sand, what if there were no oceans or distant land?

What would a mountain be if it did not rise from the sea, a poet without words what would he be.

A mind without thoughts would be a lost soul, a heart without love will pay its toll.

What would a mountain be without its peak, there would be no tops to reach or adventures to seek?

What would a poet be without the words they write, It would be like a day that has no light.

No forest no mountains no oceans and no sand, no place for you no place for me there would be no place to stand.

What would an artist be if it could not paint the birds?

What would a poet be if he could not write the words?

Without all this the world would seem odd, nothing would exist if there were no God.

No death no birth, no heavens no earth.

Written by

Rick Beyer Aloha

"The Words of An Artist"

I had this desire an artist I wish to be, I could not paint a flower, nor could I paint a tree.

I could not paint the mountains that rose into the sky, nor could I paint the rivers that continued flowing by.

I could not paint the clouds that hid the summer's sun, nor could I paint the children that were having fun.

I could not paint the plants and birds or things, nor could I paint the flowers that grow in the spring.

I could not paint the changing of the seasons, I could Not paint for any reason.

An artist I will be even if I cannot draw, I will write the words to describe what I saw.

It then became clear; in the meadow I now can see a deer.

I then saw the sun rise and then I watched it set, I then saw strangers shaking hands soon after they met.

I saw mountains rise into the sky with snow atop its peak, I then could see the fish jumping in the creek.

If a picture is worth a thousand words there must be a value to the words I write, because I paint a picture for someone to see even if they have no sight.

Written by

Rick Beyer Aloha

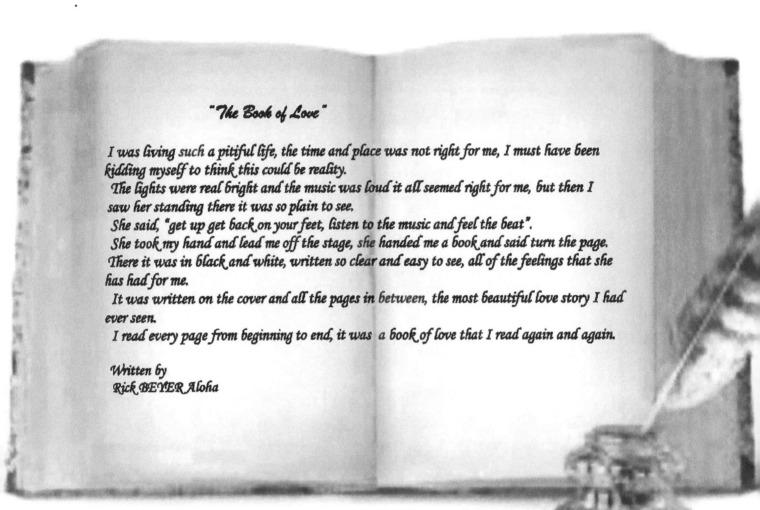

"The Book of Love"

I was living such a pitiful life, the time and place was not right for me, I must have been kidding myself to think this could be reality.

The lights were real bright and the music was loud it all seemed right for me, but then I saw her standing there it was so plain to see.

She said, "get up get back on your feet, listen to the music and feel the beat".

She took my hand and lead me off the stage, she handed me a book and said turn the page.

There it was in black and white, written so clear and easy to see, all of the feelings that she has had for me.

It was written on the cover and all the pages in between, the most beautiful love story I had ever seen.

I read every page from beginning to end, it was a book of love that I read again and again.

Written by
Rick BEYER Aloha

"A Distant Shore"

I stood upon the beach of a distant shore, beyond the horizon there are countries at war.

So hard to imagine and it's much harder to believe, peace was among us but since has been reprieved.

The water is calm the sun has risen, but soon all will change by one man's decision.

Here I stand day after day, for world peace I constantly pray.

It seems as though from this prayer we will never get a break, when one war ends another lies in its wake.

The battles are different no matter where you turn, Governments fall, and cities burn.

There's no peace among us we can't find it no more, the blood of man has washed upon a distant shore.

Written by

Rick Beyer Aloha

60

"Then And Now"

I looked back in time and saw myself as the child I was, stare back at me just because.

I tried to remember the time that past, but that was then, and the memories don't last.

One by one each grain had fallen; this is now as time came call-in.

I stared up at me now old and gray, trying my best to remember this day.

I didn't notice for the time did pass, as the sand fell through the hourglass.

Time had stolen my youth away though I don't know how, but that was then, and this is now.

Written by

Rick Beyer Aloha

"Moving The World"

If moving the world was something I had planned, I would search for the perfect place to take a stand.

My thoughts are the place where I think I'll start, because I know that I think with my heart.

I will move the world with the love that I have come to know, stand back and watch as it begins to grow.

I have taken a stand with the words I create, to move the world by declaring war on violence and hate.

We can all move the world if we take a stand, look each other in the eye and shake each other's hand.

Written by

Rick Beyer Aloha

"The Final Frontier"

After man has his final day, and all that has ever been falls to decay

Will things ever be again or has life as we know it come to an end.

The planet earth has more than one man's needs, but they will fight for it all till the last man bleeds.

They will destroy it all, until cities crumble and the last tree falls.

They will then turn towards the stars and beyond without any fear and find a way to destroy what's known as the final frontier.

Written by

Rick Beyer Aloha

"A Moment in Time"

It's been around forever it was the first of all things and it you can never regain, moments in time are here and they're gone like a summer rain.

You can carry it around in an hourglass, but still, it will never last.

Some seem to lose track of the most precious thing of all, there are moments in time that we lose that we never will recall.

There are moments that never happened stolen by a thief in the night, there is nothing that can ever happen that can make this right.

I searched among the ruins looking for the moment that was lost to some this did matter even knowing what it cost.

You can store it in the attic like memory in a box or a sack, all except for the moments in time that we will never get back.

Written by

Rick Beyer Aloha

"Trail Of Tears"

Our history of hard times is growing faint, our trails of tears were not of paint.

I am a warrior of hope and have fought great fights, I have stood on the battle fields of man that stole our rights.

Now it is all over hard times have been had, we now are living an unnatural life, tears will fall, and our people sad.

We stand on the edge of a life few will ever know, there is blood on the land that one day will no longer show.

We have sir come to the evils of man and taken from us our freedom and our land.

We have fallen to the evils of their gun; we were here in the beginning but now we are done.

Anxious we are to move on with life and live as we intended, we will live life again but not until this one has ended.

We have fought as warriors brave and strong and had no fears, only to die on the trail of tears.

Written by

Rick Beyer Aloha

"Let Me Go"

No longer will I allow him to control me the way he planned; no longer will I live in the grips of his hand.

For way to long I have been suppressed, my thoughts and my feelings were never expressed.

I will break myself free from the grips of man, and live my life the way that I plan.

I lived with it for years and often I cried, I could not break the grip no matter how hard I tried.

I have broken his grip now I am free, free from the grips that imprisoned me.

Release me from these grips for there are things I wish to know, open your hand now "Let Me Go".

Written by

Rick Beyer Aloha

"The Show Must Go On"

I stood upon the stage and pounded the keys, buildings started to crumble, and people were falling to their knees.

People were crying and others were yelling, I kept playing acting like I didn't hear the shelling.

Nations against nations the world is at war, acting like it's a game and death is how they score.

The walls have all fallen the roof has caved in, the show must go on I now will begin.

Written by

Rick Beyer Aloha

67

"My Father Cries"

As we exchange our vows you and I, in the back of my mind I can see my father cry.

His little princess I have always been, he knew one day this would come but not before his life would end.

We had our little tea parties like fathers and daughters do, how much my daddy loved me I always knew.

I have grown to be the lady he dreamed I would be, I never thought this day he would not see.

Daddy wasn't here to walk me down the aisle, so I sat, and I cried for just a little while.

I have met the man to whom I will give my hand, daddy I'm sorry you couldn't be here to give me away the way we had planned.

When I said I do I looked to the sky, and in the back of my mind I can see my father cry.

Written by

Rick Beyer Aloha

"Pier Pressure "

One by one they roll on by, while the sun is rising in the sky.

Through the pilings they come crashing to the sand, ignoring the obstacles made by man.

Fighting the pressures from the sea, peer pressure is strong as can be.

Challenges before us we must meet, pressures from our peers we must defeat.

Shall I make it and see life clear, I'll watch the sun rise through this pier

Written by

Rick Beyer Aloha

"My Return"

In my final day return me to the place I love, where I and the sand are one, let me lay here for eternity and listen to the ocean and feel the warmth of the summer sun.

Let me witness the joy of others, young and old, creating the memories when the stories are told.

Return me to the place where castles are made in the sand, and lovers young and old are walking and holding hands.

Let me lay here and watch the sun rise and set and witness the memories I'll never forget.

I will lay here where the sand and I in the ocean can churn, to the earth I shall make my return.

Written by

Rick Beyer Aloha

"THE COWBOY IN ME"

Upon the wall, I have hung my rope and under my hat I no longer stand.

I have traded my boots for a good pair of walking shoes, so I can find my way across this Barren land.

For every step, I make I will take in stride, from a top of my high horse I will no longer ride.

The cowboy in me has made a change, as I look across the open range.

My horse I have set free and I have released the spirit within me.

I will follow the wind for where it may blow, and along the way I will share the wisdom I have come to know.

Written by

Rick Beyer Aloha

"WHERE DOES TIME GO"

In a box I don't think it would stay, on a chain and in my pocket still it seems to get away.

We start looking back and we always seem to wonder where did time go, we try to remember how did it get away, sometimes we'll never know.

I start to think and then I start to see, time is catching up to me.

I look to the future to find some time, for there are still some mountains left for me to climb.

At the top it may be lonely and it may be cold, if we could only share our time, for your hand I wish to hold, because time continues and it will not stop, and we have not yet reached the top, time continue and your hand I still wish to hold.

Let's make things right, because time is running out and things are growing old, PLEASE! take my hand, there's somethings to you I'd like to show, before we ask where did the TIME GO!!!!!

Written by

Rick Beyer Aloha

"The Writing Shack"

I traveled to a far-off place, so my steps you cannot trace.

I traveled a distance that was far from here, so I can gather my thoughts and see things clear

I spent some time looking around, gathering new thoughts to write them down.

It's a place I go when I need to write, peace and quiet all day and night.

It's time to travel back to the places I know the best, after I had a well-needed rest.

I could have stayed a little longer for I have so much to write, my days grow long and my sleep I start to fight.

I have to go but I know I'll be back, because I enjoy the quiet of my writing Shack.

Written by

Rick Beyer Aloha

Printed in the USA
CPSIA information can be obtained
at www.ICGtesting.com
LVHW060758270224
772932LV00002B/25